GETTING PAID TO
Make Cosplay
Costumes and
Props

CHRISTY MIHALY

ROSEN
PUBLISHING®

New York

Published in 2017 by The Rosen Publishing Group, Inc.
29 East 21st Street, New York, NY 10010

Copyright © 2017 by The Rosen Publishing Group, Inc.

First Edition

Library of Congress Cataloging-in-Publication Data

Names: Mihaly, Christy, author.
Title: Getting paid to make cosplay costumes and props / Christy Mihaly.
Description: First edition. | New York : Rosen Publishing, 2017. | Series: Turning your tech hobbies into a career | Includes bibliographical references and index.
Identifiers: LCCN 2016023764 | ISBN 9781508173021 (library bound)
Subjects: LCSH: Cosplay—Juvenile literature. | Costume design—Vocational guidance—Juvenile literature.
Classification: LCC GV1201.8 .M54 2017 | DDC 793.93—dc23
LC record available at https://lccn.loc.gov/2016023764

Manufactured in Malaysia

Contents

Introduction

Whether you're into comic books, live action role-playing games, Disney movies, zombies, or historical reenactment, chances are you don't mind getting together with some other discerning folks who share your interest. Maybe you've gone on a zombie walk or visited a Renaissance fair. Or perhaps you're planning a trip to a fan convention, where you'll meet thousands of people celebrating their favorite characters.

A fan convention, or "con," could revolve around specific television shows or video games. Some conventions cover a whole genre, such as comic books, anime, or science fiction. But one thing is certain: when you step into a con, you'll see bustling crowds of excited fans. You may notice stars signing autographs, photographers doing shoots, and celebrities addressing excited audiences. Don't miss the dazzling decorations, artists selling their handcrafted wares, and booths selling costumes, props, and souvenirs.

But wait! Is that Nova, from *StarCraft*, strolling by? You've just spotted a fan showing off some amazing cosplay. Cosplayers work hard to re-create characters in intricate detail. Some participants spend months creating outfits and props to prepare for a convention. Cosplay goes beyond dressing up and becomes performance art. Many cosplayers step fully into character, playing their roles with serious enthusiasm. Of course, they'll be admiring other cosplayers' costumes, too. The

Fans of Marvel's *Guardians of the Galaxy* show off their costumes at Comic-Con International: San Diego in 2015. The Groot costume (*pictured right*) demonstrates advanced fabrication techniques.

excitement is electrifying—sometimes literally! Some elaborate outfits incorporate electronics and robotic parts.

A cosplayer strives to capture the exact look of a character. Cosplayers research the characters they want to portray. They'll consult photographs and drawings. They'll re-create that look with costumes and props made of fabric, metal, cardboard, thermoplastics, or lightweight foam. They'll seek out the perfect makeup for the character and a wig to get the hair just right. A cosplayer's look might require body paint or sparkles, temporary tattoos, colored contact lenses, or other special effects. And that's just for starters!

Many cosplayers construct accessories and props to complete their presentation. This could mean jewelry or space-age weapons. Some build models of alien creatures, vehicles, or robots. These models may be simple or elaborate. And they may be crafted by hand or generated with a 3D printer.

Cosplayers travel to conventions in Japan, Russia, the Philippines, Canada, and all over the world. They do this because they enjoy the creativity and camaraderie of sharing their passion.

But cosplayers also develop a solid set of practical skills. They need to know how to organize, budget, sew, and fabricate. Cosplay often also involves collaborating with others and entering competitions.

So read on to get the scoop about where to learn what you need to know for cosplay, whether it's happening in school, online, or elsewhere. Discover cosplay technology tips. And find out how cosplay skills—used to re-create an imaginary world— can help you achieve real-world success.

Chapter ONE

Bringing Characters to Life with Costumes and Props

The word "cosplay" derives from "costume" and "play." Cosplay mixes these two things. It usually involves re-creating a specific character or historical figure. It's difficult to define "cosplay" precisely, though, because this is a hobby that continues to grow and evolve.

SCI-FI BEGINNINGS: BACK TO THE FUTURE

Science fiction stories and movies, in which science is joined with fantasy or fiction, became increasingly popular in the 1920s and 1930s. Growing audiences enjoyed books, films, and comic books about humanlike robots, spaceships, and fantastic alien beings. In those days before the internet, when fans wanted

Forty years after he and Myrtle Jones brought cosplay to the world, Forrest Ackerman displays his replica of a robot from a 1926 sci-fi film at his home.

to get together to discuss their science fiction interests, they organized sci-fi conventions.

At the 1939 World Science Fiction Convention (WorldCon) in New York City, science fiction fans Myrtle R. Jones and Forrest Ackerman showed up in costume. They wore futuristic, sci-fi-inspired outfits with satin capes, which Jones had designed and constructed. They made quite a splash.

Convention costuming caught on. At the 1940 WorldCon, many participants wore costumes. In the 1940s and 1950s, attendance grew. Some cons held masquerades for attendees to show off their costumes. Many fans dressed as superheroes and supervillains, such as DC Comics' Superman and Lex Luthor. When the CBS television series *Star Trek* took off in the 1960s, Trekkies showed up dressed as characters from the Starship *Enterprise*. Fans of Japanese anime and manga and those of British sci-fi such as the BBC's *Doctor Who* soon joined the party. As new fandoms arose, conventions welcomed X-Philes, Potterheads, Tolkienites, Star Warriors, Marvelites, and more.

Today, cosplay has spread around the globe. Cosplayers come from diverse backgrounds, and they're interested in everything from ancient history to the far future. What these fans have in common is their devotion to their craft, combining serious study with crazy creativity.

WHO ARE YOU SUPPOSED TO BE?

Cosplayers have a wide universe of possible costumes to choose from. As individuals or in groups, cosplayers may portray characters from a variety of genres. Here's a quick run-down of some popular cosplay subjects.

A pair of Harry Potter fans gets into the spirit and into costume at a California bookstore event celebrating the release of *Harry Potter and the Deathly Hallows.*

SCIENCE FICTION, FANTASY, AND HORROR

Science fiction includes shows and movies such as *Star Trek*, *Star Wars*, and *Blade Runner*. Cosplayers may portray the human or nonhuman stars of these stories or minor characters. Some cosplayers represent generic characters such as the storm troopers from *Star Wars*. People also cosplay characters from horror flicks or apocalyptic tales or cartoon characters from Disney movies. They may find their inspiration anywhere from *Harry Potter* to *Twilight* to *Game of Thrones*.

Living History: Another Kind of Cosplay?

Historical reenactments enable history buffs to live for a short time like people from days gone by. Members of the Society for Creative Anachronism (SCA), for example, practice the arts and crafts of the Middle Ages. Participants in the SCA are organized by kingdom, and may choose medieval names and personas. Members attired in tunics and hose attend tournaments featuring jousting events on horseback, archery competitions, ax throwing, medieval banquets, and more. Some may participate in Renaissance fairs, where fairgoers dressed in Elizabethan costume meet Queen Elizabeth I as strolling musicians play music from the sixteenth century.

Other historian hobbyists delve into other time periods. Some specialize in re-creating the clothing and armor of the ancient Romans. Others are interested in the mountain men of the American West or specific local historical figures. They all work to bring history to life, for participants and spectators alike.

Some history enthusiasts re-create historic battles. In the United States, thousands of American Civil War reenactors, dressed in blue or gray Civil War uniforms,

(continued on the next page)

(continued from the previous page)

stage historically accurate—though less deadly— reenactments of actual battles. Reenactors strive for authenticity in their dress, weapons, and battle plans. Interested groups present battles from the American Revolution to recent conflicts.

Some consider historical reenactment distinct from cosplay. Reenactors may prefer to call their hobby living history. But historical reenactment, like cosplay, requires diligent research and preparation, and its participants enjoy creating authentic costumes and getting into character.

ANIME AND MANGA

Some conventions specialize in the distinctive Japanese art forms of manga and anime. But at many different cons, you'll see cosplayers dressed as Pokémon creatures or characters from anime or manga comics and animation, including *Sailor Moon* and *Cowboy Bebop*, and many more.

SUPERHEROES AND SUPERVILLAINS

Conventions usually feature many cosplayers dressed as characters from Marvel Comics, such as Captain Marvel or Wolverine, and DC Comics' Batman or Wonder Woman. You'll also see swarms of the colorful criminals that these heroes are known to combat.

Chat with a Teen Cosplayer

Caroline Donahue likes *Star Wars,* Disney movies, *My Little Pony,* and Marvel Comics' *Jessica Jones, X-Men,* and *The Avengers.* She began cosplaying at age thirteen.

Q: How did you get started with cosplay?
A: I learned about conventions from fan websites. Then, in 2014, I attended Bronycon. That's the big convention for bronies, [people who are] *My Little Pony* fans. Seeing all those costumes made me want to cosplay.

Q: What was your first costume?
A: I wanted a variation on a Pony character, so I was Pirate Pinkie Pie. I wore a pink corset and wig, a pirate hat, and eye patch. I carried a sword that I'd spray-painted pink. I didn't make everything from scratch, but it turned out great. I entered the cosplay contest at Midwest Bronyfest. I thought it would be scary, but it was just fun.

Q: What do you like about cosplay?
A: It allows you to be a completely different person. It boosts your bravery. Also, cosplayers put so much creativity into their costumes. I've seen princess gowns or suits of armor that took maybe a year of work in someone's garage.

(continued on the next page)

(continued from the previous page)

I'm more of a last-minute person. Lots of us are in our hotel rooms the day before the contest, hot-gluing our costumes together. That's part of the fun, too.

I've met great people at conventions. You make friends because you're all doing something you love.

Q: Is there anything you dislike about cosplay?
A: Sometimes those costumes are itchy and hot. But it's worth it!

Q: What's next?
A: Another convention, if I convince my parents. In 2015, I cosplayed Scientist Twilight Sparkle. I'm thinking about being Rey from *Star Wars* or Jessica Jones.

Q: What's your advice to newbies?
A: Just don't be afraid!

GAMING

Gaming fans may enjoy cosplaying a favorite character from a video or role-playing game. If you're a fan of Nintendo's *Super Mario Brothers*, why not cosplay Mario or Princess Peach? If you're more into *Dungeons & Dragons*, how about a cosplay of your D&D player character? Or if that's not your style, pick any royalty, ninja, or villain from your game of choice.

MASH-UPS

Creative cosplayers combine disparate characters or themes into an original costume. How about a zombie starship commander or a steampunk superhero? It's up to you.

GOOD TO GO

Creating a costume and props requires planning and work. Have you identified a convention or other gathering you'd like

Before you start sewing your costume, take time to prepare. Collect the tools and materials you'll need, such as fabric, shears, and measuring tape.

to attend in costume? If so, here are four basic steps to get your cosplay started.

Step one: research and design.

Cosplay usually involves replicating an existing character, so planning a costume starts with research. This means collecting photographs and other images of the character in different poses. You'll design your costume based on these images.

When you have a clear idea of your cosplay look, compile a wish list of what you'd like to include in your costume and props. What materials do you need? Will you wear a wig? Do you want colored contact lenses or body paint? Would you love your costume or props to include lights or electronic gadgets?

To refine your materials list, visit stores—online and in real life—to compare fabrics, craft supplies, and other equipment, including the prices. Here's where step two comes in.

Step two: work within your budget.

You'll probably hear about a cosplayer who spent more than $1,000 to make some complicated, fully functional, ten-foot (three-meter) Optimus Prime. That might be impressive, but you'll need to stick to a reasonable budget for your cosplay. First, calculate the admission fees and the costs of getting to the convention, as well as paying for extras such as photos, autographs, and other souvenirs. Then you can figure out how much money remains for the construction or purchase of your costume and props—or, plan to earn more money before the convention! If you're tech oriented, there are programs or apps to help you organize your cosplay budget. Cosplanner or Goodbudget are good options.

Now look at your materials list, and compare your estimated costs with your available cash. Can you save on expenses by borrowing or recycling? Is there a freecycle network in your area? Look for places near you that sell or give away reclaimed or reused supplies, and check on Craigslist and bulletin boards. If you're creative, you'll find many ways to save.

Step three: make a schedule.

To assure you'll finish your work by the convention, you'll want to plan your time. You could use a timetable on a smartphone, an online calendar, or a paper notebook. List each step for the construction of your costume and props. Estimate how long each step will take. Do you have to order supplies? How long will it take to cut the pieces for your armor? Do you need to allow extra time to take lessons in a new fabrication technique? Allow time for errors and setbacks, too.

Committing yourself to complete a certain task by a certain date helps you know if you're on schedule. You may think it sounds like fun to be hot-gluing your costume in your hotel room the night before the cosplay competition. But if you can finish your work before you head to the con, you'll probably be glad you did.

Step four: make it so!

Once you've refined your lists, it's time to hit neighborhood garage sales, thrift stores, scrap yards, freecycle locations, and the like. Check eBay and online suppliers, too. Gather those raw materials, and start crafting!

If you already know how to craft or sew, you've got a head start. If not, the next chapter provides ideas about where to learn the skills. For example, there may be a makerspace or Fab Lab (fabrication laboratory) in your school or library. Makerspaces provide craft and hardware supplies and tools and are often staffed by people who can explain how to use the equipment. The internet also offers a wealth of resources, including costume and prop-making tutorials, podcasts, and

When looking for quirky, fun, and affordable costume pieces, don't forget to check out the racks of neighborhood thrift stores.

cosplay forums. Perhaps you can find an established costuming or cosplay group in your area, or join an online group.

If the costume you envisioned turns out to be too complicated, simplify it, and defer the more elaborate cosplay until you've had some practice. Just remember, as cosplayer Caroline says, "Don't be afraid." Going to a convention in a cool costume is a great way to make friends and build your own cosplay community.

Chapter TWO

Schools and Tools for Cosplay

Whether you're just starting out in cosplay or are looking to improve your game, there are plenty of places to find instruction and support. Do you want to learn to sew? Need practice with computer-aided design or help creating a web-shooter for your superhero cosplay? Want to create a compelling website to advertise your costumes? There's a class for that!

GETTING CLASSY AT SCHOOL

Start by checking out classes and activities at your school. The required curriculum of English, history, science, and math can help with cosplay. You'll need decent math skills (especially geometry!) for measuring and designing costumes and props, and you'll want to be comfortable with numbers when you're creating budgets and business plans. If you're interested in building robots, pay attention in physics class. And history and English can provide great background and inspiration for cosplay.

Studying in school and taking on additional courses available online or in the community can help you make your cosplay classier and more well-informed.

In addition, in many districts, you can sign up for vocational and arts courses such as sewing, welding, construction, and computer-aided design. Here's a run-down of specialized subjects from A to Z that can make you a better-educated cosplayer. You'll probably think of even more.

ART

In art, you can study color theory, art history, and design. Art classes can improve your drawing, painting, and design techniques. Some schools' art departments also include advanced or technical subjects such as computer graphics and drafting.

Your school newspaper might need someone to supply art or photographs. Many publications need people to help with layout and graphic design and distribution. Outside of school, perhaps you can find a small local publication or newsletter that would be thrilled to have an intern assisting the staff with graphic design or other tasks.

BUSINESS

Cosplay isn't just about making stuff; it's about organizing the stuff. If you want to make money with cosplay, you'll need to know how to operate the business end of things. Look for courses about how to start and run a business. Knowledge of accounting, marketing, and time management can come in handy.

Some schools and community centers host youth business clubs. These clubs can work with local businesses and give you practice in applying business principles. Sometimes they coordinate with local nonprofit organizations. If your community or school doesn't offer this option, perhaps you can suggest it!

COMPUTER SCIENCE

Perhaps a course in computer programming is a good choice for you. In some classes, you can brush up on how to create spreadsheets and slide shows or learn graphic design and desktop publishing programs. In others, you'll design websites or computer games. Or you can take part in a computer-aided design (CAD) course. CAD software enables you to design complex, three-dimensional objects with a computer. With 3D printing, you can print these shapes in three dimensions, using different materials. CAD courses teach you how to produce precision drawings and 3D models.

CONSTRUCTION TRADES

Courses in auto mechanics, welding, electrical work, and woodworking can all come in handy in constructing props and complex costumes. You'll learn how to work with different

A group of acting students at the National Institute of Dramatic Art in Sydney, Australia rehearse for a play.

materials, how to design and plan projects, and how to create special effects with paints and finishes. You can learn the principles of engines and electricity. Knowing your way around a workshop, and which tools to use for which jobs, will give you an edge in bringing your cosplay designs to life.

DRAMA

Cosplay can include an element of acting, so why not check out a drama class? Drama programs not only train students to act, they often cover skills needed for designing sets, creating costumes and props, and directing the show.

Similarly, offering to help with the school play can land you a role in acting or in designing or constructing costumes, props, and sets. Or, you can learn to manage these activities. Community musical and dramatic productions also frequently need interns or volunteers. Putting on a play requires many hands.

FAMILY AND CONSUMER SCIENCES, SEWING, AND DESIGN

Some schools offer courses in family and consumer sciences (formerly—and sometimes still—called home economics). These classes vary widely, but may include hand sewing, machine sewing, embroidery, design, and other skills useful in making costumes, as well as other clothes.

FASHION DESIGN

Courses in fashion design can show you how to create patterns for garment making, both manually and using computers. You'll learn how to handle various textiles and other materials, such as leather and metal. Look for training in illustration and computer graphics here, too.

FILM HISTORY

In film studies or a class on the history of movies, you could study the techniques and the historical significance of the great films and great directors, expanding your understanding of this visual art form.

Many advanced cosplay props and costumes incorporate robotic parts. If you're interested, consider looking into a robotics class or club to learn about making and operating robots.

PHOTOGRAPHY

If you want to take more eye-catching photos, consider a photography course. Many cosplayers pose for professional photographs in costume, and they're looking for somebody talented on the other side of that camera. Take a class to learn about composing and shooting pictures and developing the film. Familiarity with digital editing to add exotic backgrounds and special effects can come in handy in cosplay photography.

ROBOTICS

If you have the math and science background and interest, look for a course in robotics, in which you can design and build robotic devices. From gears and motors to electronics and autonomous programming, robotics covers it all.

If there's a robotics club or computer club in your school or community, check it out. These groups learn about programming and building robots. Some compete in robotics games against other teams.

FINDING ENLIGHTENMENT ELSEWHERE

If your school doesn't offer the courses you want, don't give up. Look for classes outside of school, starting with the options mentioned below. Or, look for something other than classes. You can learn a great deal outside of formal courses. For example, you could join a group that works on issues of interest to you. You might get some valuable experience through an internship or by volunteering to help a local organization. You can create possibilities wherever you find something that interests you.

COLLEGES

Check to see if a community college or other institution near you offers public workshops or courses that are open to high school students. These may be free, or scholarships may be available for qualified applicants. Or perhaps you could audit a class (attend a class without receiving credit).

COMMUNITY CENTERS

In cities and towns large and small, community members share their expertise in classes and workshops. Topics range from photography to sewing, computer programming to accounting, and poetry to drawing. Perhaps your local recreation department, gym, or house of worship offers interesting courses.

INDEPENDENT STUDIES

If your school has an independent study program, consider taking advantage of it. Independent study often involves working closely with a specific teacher and/or a community mentor on a project of your own design. If you are clear about your learning goals, and you can identify a person you'd like to work with in your field of interest, you might be a good candidate for an independent study.

ONLINE COURSES

The internet abounds with learning opportunities. You'll find many video tutorials on YouTube and elsewhere. These cover subjects from CAD to crafting. You'll find people teaching fashion,

Publishing a school or community newspaper or magazine takes teamwork. Members of the team cover writing, photography, layout, and other tasks.

photography, and foam props. You can also check out the Khan Academy, whose free online offerings include computer science and coding classes. In addition, Lynda.com and other sites offer online business and computer classes for a fee. Just remember: before paying for online courses, check the reviews thoroughly to confirm the provider is reputable and reliable.

Fab Labs and Makerspaces

When you have an idea for a project you want to make yourself, but you don't have the tools, materials, or knowledge you need, where can you go? Look for a makerspace or Fab Lab in your area! These kinds of facilities might also be called a hackerspace, hacklab, or tech shop where you live.

A makerspace is a space where you make things! Makerspaces are often stocked with computers, 3D printers, sewing machines, art and craft supplies, and other equipment for turning your brilliant ideas into reality. They may offer supplies for electrical wiring and digital electronics, various metals, wood, and foam supplies. They may have tools including saws, machine drills, and CNC routers (computer-controlled cutters). They're often located in schools or public libraries, museums, and in and around college campuses.

And in addition to technology, at these places you'll find other people making things. There's often an expert staff, as well as other makers willing to show less experienced crafters how things work. In these community spaces, makers can share their knowledge, their models, and their enthusiasm about making things themselves.

ON-THE-JOB TRAINING

One of the best ways to pick up new skills is on-the-job training. Being paid to learn—how cool is that? If you need a job and you want to learn, look for a place where you can pick up some cosplay-related skills while earning a paycheck. And if your dream employer isn't hiring, consider offering to work for free or seeking out an unpaid internship. Sometimes that can lead to paying work.

SALES

If you think you'd like to work at a cash register, why not head for a job in a bookstore, a craft or sewing shop, a comic book store, or a costume shop? How about a clothing outlet, where you may also be able to do alterations for customers? Or a store that sells toys or models relating to your cosplay interests? In a retail post, you can brush up on your people skills and practical math. You can learn about the merchandise, and you'll have access to information about events such as author visits, craft fairs, fashion shows, and conventions. And you could get a nice employee discount.

SEWING

If you know how to sew, you might seek a paid apprenticeship or job at a sewing or craft shop. Mending and tailoring jobs may not be easy to find, but if you don't look, you won't know what openings are out there. Some theater companies pay for costuming work, and that can also be terrific experience.

If you're technology-oriented, working as a part-time technical support specialist can offer you training and experience in communications and customer service.

TECHNOLOGY SUPPORT

If you're technology savvy, a job in technical support could present you with many interesting issues. You could get valuable experience from solving customers' information technology problems. Or perhaps your local Fab Lab needs some more staff.

If you can't find a job, try creating your own. Many technology professionals earn money by advertising their services, such as debugging laptops, helping seniors learn to use their smartphones, or improving cybersecurity for local businesses.

Chapter THREE

What It Takes to Cosplay: The Skills You Need

Making costumes and props requires skill, but cosplay is open to all. Your first costume doesn't have to be perfect. Every expert cosplayer started as a beginner, and the cosplay community supports people at all levels. That said, developing some of the skills described in this chapter will help you boost the level of your cosplay.

BEGIN WITH THE BASICS

There are so many cons every year that a cosplayer will have abundant opportunity to display his or her work or find inspiration. This is good news because it means that there is plenty of time to refine the abilities that one needs.

Comic books can be helpful reference materials for character research, especially since every character in them has a distinct look.

DOING RESEARCH

Cosplay starts with studying your character. You'll investigate and determine the details of a costume you want to make. Much of this research can be done on the internet.

SEWING AND EMBROIDERY

Most costumes are stitched from fabric, by hand with a needle and thread, or with a sewing machine. Many books and courses teach sewing skills. Sewing machines make the process faster, but you have to learn to use them, and they range in complexity. Digital sewing machines can be programmed to do embroidery or other fancy stitches and finishes.

CRAFTING WITH VARIOUS MATERIALS

Costumes may incorporate many materials. Spandex, sparkles, beads, wood, clay, metal, polyurethane foam, leather, plastic, resins, feathers—costumes are created with all these and more. Costumers develop familiarity with manipulating different materials. They learn which type of thread to use with which fabric; which glue works for wood and which for plastic, and what kind of feathers are best.

PAINTING

For props and armor and some fabric costumes, cosplayers need to know about different kinds of paint and painting techniques. Some costumes involve shading, highlighting, detail work, and weathering for a realistic finish. It's often much more than just stitching together wood, plastic, and fabrics.

BEYOND THE BASICS: COMPLETING THE LOOK

At conventions and cosplay meet-ups, you might see stunning cosplay by experts who have mastered advanced fabrication techniques. If you ask, experienced cosplayers are often willing to share the secrets of how they made their creations. Here are some advanced cosplay highlights.

A fan gets assistance with her makeup at a 2012 anime convention in Hong Kong. Many cosplayers use cosmetics to more closely match their characters' appearance.

MAKEUP

Like actors in movies or plays, cosplayers rely on cosmetics to create their characters. A cosplayer pays attention to facial details, including the eyebrows, skin color, and scars of the character he or she wants to represent. False eyelashes and false eyebrows (to match the wig!) are often used in cosplay. More advanced techniques include realistic-looking latex scars, which can be fashioned with liquid latex, then colored with makeup. And some cosplayers use contact lenses that make their eyes look silver or red or otherwise otherworldly.

HAIR AND WIGS

Many cosplayers wear wigs rather than trying to arrange their own hair to match a character. This is especially true when cosplaying anime and manga and other characters with green or pink spikes. Wigs let you experiment with wild cuts or long, flowing tresses. Some cosplayers dye and style their own wigs. Wig styling is different from hair styling because wigs are synthetic and not structured like real hair. The internet is full of tutorials on how to style, and even make, wigs.

BODY PAINT AND TEMPORARY TATTOOS

Many cosplayers learn to make their own temporary tattoos. One method is to draw a tattoo design on tracing paper with gel pens. To cosplay a character whose skin tone doesn't match the cosplayer's natural skin, many cosplayers use body paint (and/or face paint). Whether it's vampire white, demon red, or alien green, body paint can strengthen a cosplay presentation.

Starting Suggestions

1. **Start small and simple.** Start with a simple costume and props. Most cosplayers begin with easy costumes. They make mistakes and they learn from their experience. If you're not an expert at sewing or crafting, can you put something together with duct tape? Or you could ditch the complete outfit, and just wear some distinctive accessories: a mask, a cape, a medallion, or a hat.

2. **Ask for help.** Cosplayers learn by doing and asking questions. Help is available online on social media and websites where cosplayers exchange information about materials, supplies, designs, and techniques. Maybe friends or family members can answer your questions about how to make something. Just ask!

3. **Consider alternatives.** Sometimes you'll need to come up with a substitute, or a less expensive material. Don't worry about your costume not being perfect because nobody's is. You could even buy a costume. Although most cosplayers make their own, if you'd rather not, don't sweat it.

4. **Wear comfortable shoes.** People who break this rule live to regret it. Most cosplay, especially at conventions, requires walking, lots of walking.

5. **Have fun!** Cosplay involves challenging yourself to see what cool creation you can come up with. But cosplay is fundamentally about dressing up as a character you love, for the joy of it, and seeing other people smile with you. So enjoy yourself.

SHOES

Yes, those shoes should be comfortable. But you probably won't want to wear your old running shoes. One option is to make fabric shoe covers, which pull over your comfy shoes and match the costume's fabric. Another tip from the experts: have two pairs of shoes, and carry those spectacular costume shoes to put on just before competition or photography sessions.

CASTS AND MOLDING

Some cosplayers take casts of their heads to allow for custom molding of costume and prop pieces. A mold of the cosplayer's head will allow a custom headpiece or horns to be sculpted to fit his or her head and face precisely. More elaborate techniques may involve crafting facial ridges or bony structures to portray nonhuman characters.

GETTING DRAMATIC

Cosplayers don't just dress up, they often speak and move "in character." So although it's not strictly required, a flair for the dramatic, and a willingness to do a bit of acting, can be an advantage.

TACKLING THE TECHNOLOGY

You'll find a great deal of high-tech power in cosplay, both behind the scenes and out front on display. Some cosplayers go all out and build replicas of giant, motorized robots, while others use smaller-scale electronics such as strings of lights to enhance a costume. Cosplayers also use technology for design and construction.

At a 2013 competition in Indonesia, a cosplayer in full armor portrays the Emperor from *Armor Hero*, a Chinese science fiction series.

One area of increasing interest is 3D modeling. For example, with Pepakura software, you can make cutout models from paper or cardstock to design and construct props such as helmets and armor. CAD programs such as Tinkercad or Blender allow you to build 3D models on the computer and translate them into being with a 3D printer.

Avoid Online Offensiveness

On cosplay forums and social media, as is true elsewhere on the internet, you may run across inappropriate comments and hostile remarks. Here are some quick reminders about keeping the internet friendly and safe.

DON'T TALK TO TROLLS:
- Don't get sucked into lengthy exchanges with rude commenters. The only exception to this advice is that sometimes it can make sense to post a single, public, factual response to provide corrections and counteract lies in a comment. Then, let it go.
- Report inappropriate comments to the moderator or the appropriate social media channels to block the troll.

PROTECT YOURSELF:
- Don't provide your full name, phone number, or address to anyone you don't know or trust.
- Think twice before you post photos or let others take pictures of you, in or out of costume. Photos can be shared and retweeted, and once your image is out there, it's beyond your control.
- If you receive offensive comments, take a screenshot to save as documentation, just in case you later decide to ask the police for help.

KEEP IT FUN:
- In your own online interactions, be respectful and kind toward your fellow travelers. Do your part to create a positive online atmosphere.

Sewing can also be high-tech. Electronic sewing machines can be programmed to perform complex functions and embroidery. Many costumes rely on intricate patterns of decoration for which this programming is important. You'll also find other specialized sewing attachments and machines that can improve the quality of your costumes. A serger, for example, uses numerous needles and threads to produce professional-looking finished seams.

Many of the most spectacular cosplay costumes and props use LEDs, wearable technology, and other digital devices. Constructing these costumes requires knowledge of wiring, soldering, and electronics. Makerspaces and Fab Labs can help with these projects. If you have a great idea but can't find a makerspace and don't have the equipment to turn your concept into a finished product, you might look for a digital fabricator. Through a "matchmaking" website, such as 100kGarages.com, you could locate a local business or craftsperson with the high-tech equipment you need.

Digital photography is another tech-oriented aspect of cosplay. Many cosplayers want photos of themselves in costume. They may prefer digitally enhanced effects and backgrounds to make those photographs pop. Specialists in cosplay photography know how to do digital editing.

YOUR MISSION, SHOULD YOU CHOOSE TO ACCEPT IT

If you're interested in earning money from cosplay, you'll need more than great construction skills. Once you've researched your character, created your costume, built your props, and completed your makeup and accessories, then it's time to get the word out about your work. That's when you put on your networking hat, and get down to business.

BE A COMMUNICATOR: WORKING THE NETWORK

The larger fan conventions attract many thousands of fans. Smaller crowds gather at more specialized conventions or local meet-ups. Each gathering is a chance to meet plenty of people—people who *love* cosplay. These could be new friends. They could be future mentors or future customers or clients. They're good people to know!

As you gain experience and build a portfolio, you'll want to start promoting your costumes and props at conventions. You can do this online, too. You could set up a website or blog to showcase your work. You could join cosplay groups on social media to share your works in progress and compare ideas and plans. Sharing your creativity with an appreciative audience is an important part of cosplay.

MISSION CONTROL: ORGANIZING THE STUFF

You know it's important to track the various elements of your cosplay, such as materials, schedules, makeup, and accessories. You can use spreadsheets to track these. If you decide to undertake a group cosplay with friends, the organizational challenges multiply. Group chats and online worksheets and calendars can help keep everyone up to date on the progress of a multiplayer project. These cloud-based tools make it easy to coordinate, even when group members are located in different cities or countries.

A group of cosplayers shows off different interpretations of the heroic character Link from Nintendo's *The Legend of Zelda* game series at MAGfest in 2015.

Keeping things organized will help ensure that you have all the costume and prop pieces you need when you need them. Don't let a lost part ruin your fun! Later on, attention to detail will be a big advantage in the workplace, whether you launch your own cosplay business or explore other cosplay-related careers.

Chapter FOUR

Ideas for Careers in Cosplay

Do you want to live, sleep, eat, and breathe cosplay? Or would you just like to earn some extra cash from this fun hobby? Creative cosplayers have found many ways to make cosplay pay.

FULL-TIME COSPLAY

Most cosplayers don't have full-time careers in cosplay. But for those who do, it's a dream come true. Perhaps one of these options is a good fit for you.

COSTUMES AND PROPS

Some cosplayers have turned costuming and prop making into successful businesses. For example, Holly Conrad and Jessica Merizan were middle school friends who started cosplaying together in 2007. This cosplay pair hosted the Nerdist Channel podcast *Try This At Home* and has posted many instructional videos on YouTube. In 2010, they founded a business, Crabcat Industries, to make and sell cosplay costumes. They've expanded to create monsters, masks, and other props for movies and commercials.

At the 2009 Blizzcon in Anaheim, California, German cosplayer Svetlana Quindt is modeling a *World of Warcraft* costume that she made.

Cosplayer Bill Doran also started his own business, Punished Props. He takes commissions, or special orders, to build detailed armor, replica weapons, elaborate masks and helmets, and other masterpieces. He has spoken at numerous conventions and written several books explaining his fabrication techniques.

TEACHING COSPLAY

Many cosplayers create instructional videos and how-to books. Svetlana Quindt, who lives in Germany, had been cosplaying for about ten years when she decided to start writing books about how she made cosplay costumes and props. Her business, Kamui Cosplay, sells books and she leads workshops on various fabrication techniques.

Japanese cosplayer Goldy Marg has taught classes and workshops in Tokyo and elsewhere, showing students from many countries his techniques for constructing detailed armor costumes. He's a recognized expert who has judged cosplay competitions. A long-time cosplayer himself, he particularly enjoys the intercultural exchange of cosplay.

RUNNING A COMMUNITY WEBSITE

Many cosplayers are involved in internet businesses. In 2002, photographer Kyle Johnson started his website after noticing that there was no community website for cosplayers. He established Cosplay.com to fill that need. Although he initially wondered whether he'd have five hundred members in a year, he got that many in the first month. Before long, he was working full-time on the website. Today, hundreds of thousands have joined Cosplay.com. Members can post photos and advertisements, review event listings, and join forum discussions.

Cosplay and Good Causes Around the World

Jenna "Song of Amazon" Lindeke Heavenrich started cosplaying at sixteen. After earning two graduate degrees and traveling extensively, she now lives and works in Japan. She's a longtime member of the Rebel Legion, a Lucasfilm-sanctioned *Star Wars* costuming community that participates in charity events such as hospital visits and walk-a-thons. Lindeke Heavenrich's cosplay complements her career and other interests.

Q: How did you start cosplaying?
A: After years of helping my mom sew Halloween costumes, I started cosplaying anime in high school. Then some friends asked me to costume a *Lord of the Rings* fan film. In college, I joined a performance group that re-created *Sailor Moon* dance numbers.

My cosplay also got me a great job at the costume shop for my college's theater, dance, and opera programs. I worked there for four years, which really strengthened my knowledge of sewing and the quality of my construction. About eight years ago, I started making *Star Wars* costumes for the Rebel Legion, where I now hold two global-level leadership positions.

Q: How does cosplay support your work and other interests?
A: My career centers on the nonprofit sector in international relations, international development, and peace. Cosplay complements this work. With Rebel Legion, I can use

costuming to raise money for good causes. As a Rebel Legion officer, I interact with many people from different countries. The intercultural skills I've picked up at work have made me very good at helping people with their questions, even when we don't have much vocabulary in common.

The international nature of the Rebel Legion and the cosplay community means that almost wherever I go, I have instant friends.

PROFESSIONAL COSPLAYER

What's a professional cosplayer? Cosplayer Yaya Han gets paid to cosplay. At conventions around the world, she earns fees for teaching costuming workshops and judging costume competitions, among other things. She has continued to design and make her own intricately detailed costumes and also written books and created her own brand of cosplay merchandise. Han has said that when she began to cosplay, she didn't know how to sew and could afford only a used $40 sewing machine. Now she makes a living cosplaying.

COSPLAY-RELATED OCCUPATIONS

If a full-time cosplay gig isn't your thing, you can still put your cosplay talents to work. Check out these ideas for using cosplay-related skills to make a living—on your own or working for an employer who values your cosplay credentials.

ACTING

Some cosplayers participate in anime shows, musical theater, videos, film, or performance art. Some turn to careers in these fields. One Japanese cosplayer, Akira Konomi, caught the attention of the producers of an anime show. Based on her cosplay, they hired her as a voice actor for an animated character.

ART, CARTOONING, AND ANIMATION

Consider a career in comic book art or graphic design or even digital animation. Cosplayers' understanding of costumes and fabrics can help them generate realistic-looking clothes on animated figures.

COSTUMED CHARACTERS

Some job descriptions require workers to dress in costume. At theme parks, costumed workers entertain and interact with visitors while in character. Sports teams use costumed mascots. Event-hosting companies sometimes provide costumed hosts and hostesses for promotional gatherings and special occasions. Having cosplay on your resume could help you snag one of these fun assignments.

COMPUTER MODELING AND DIGITAL TECHNOLOGY

Familiarity with 3D modeling and CAD programs is a must if you want to be an engineer or architect. That digital experience could also come in handy in many other careers, from game development to jewelry design.

Illustrator Jason Meents draws comic book characters at his studio in Colorado Springs, Colorado. Graphic design and digital animation are some other ways to pursue an interest in art.

CRAFTING, SEWING, AND FABRICATION

If you have samples of jaw-dropping props you've made, why not use them to impress someone looking for skilled craftspeople? A portfolio of handcrafted costumes can be great advertising for your sewing prowess. Or maybe wig making is your thing. If you want to put those special skills to work outside of cosplay, think about the crafty careers you might enjoy.

Designing costumes can provide a good foundation to create cutting-edge fashion. This fashion designer is using her imagination and creativity to sketch original outfits.

FASHION DESIGN

Some cosplayers may be able to carry their portfolios of beautifully crafted, fantastical costumes into the world of fashion design. Others may focus on designing jewelry or other accessories. Cosplay can provide useful experience as well as a potential customer base for these fashion-forward products.

GAME DESIGN

How about designing video games on your own or as part of a team? Gaming companies need people with the skills to code and create online games, educational products, interactive games, and more.

INTERNATIONAL OPPORTUNITIES

Many cosplayers enjoy the international aspect of cosplay. Cosplayers develop an understanding of people of different cultures and can make friends with people from around the world. Having international friends may open up international opportunities.

MODELS AND STYLISTS

Cosplay is like modeling in costume. This background may be helpful in pursuing a career as a fashion model, a product model for a promotional company, or a spokesperson for trade events. Or you may be interested in a related occupation, such as hair stylist or makeup artist.

PHOTOGRAPHY

There is a steady demand for cosplay photographers. Some smart cosplayers have started freelance cosplay photography businesses. Many also do other types of photography or have other jobs. Andrew Michael Phillips, for example, was an established fashion and portrait photographer as well as a longtime comics fan. When he first saw cosplay costumes, he was so impressed that he knew he wanted to get into photographing cosplayers.

Connecting at the Convention

If you go to a convention, you'll primarily want to enjoy the scene. But if you're looking to build a cosplay career, remember that conventions are also great places to network. Here are three top tips for making great con connections:

1. **Carry cards.** Handing a card to someone you just met makes it easy for him or her to find you later on social media. You can design cards online and have them delivered or print them yourself. Include images of you or your art and your online contact information.

2. **Venture to volunteer.** Did you know there's a way to get free admission, plus an inside view of the con and maybe even the chance to meet a celebrity? Be a convention volunteer and help run the show! Volunteers provide tech support, run photo booths, moderate panel discussions, sit at information desks, pick up convention speakers from the airport, and clean up after the con is over. A first-time volunteer probably won't be assigned to drive a big star to the airport, but volunteers are involved in behind-the-scenes logistics that ordinary congoers never see. You'll want to research the volunteer requirements and find out what you might miss if you're stuck at a volunteer post. But if it sounds like a good deal to you, sign up before the con.

3. **Follow the feed.** Follow and comment on the convention's social media feed. During the con, doing this will help you keep track of what's happening when, which long lines to avoid, and where to find the folks you want to meet.

WRITING AND PRODUCING

If writing is your thing, perhaps a graphic novel is in your future! Or your cosplay experience might help you in writing for television or movies. Television writer and producer Jane Espenson has worked on shows including *Buffy the Vampire Slayer* and *Battlestar Galactica.* In an interview in *The Fangirl's Guide to the Galaxy*, Espenson gave this career advice: "Look into ways to turn what you love into something that can become a support to you in more ways than one. I wasn't content with watching shows—I was itching to get behind the scenes and found a way to do it."

WHAT NEXT?

You can't just apply for a great job at Colossal Cosplay Corporation, Inc. Cosplay is a new and evolving art form in which people make their own opportunities. Here are four thoughts to keep in mind as you move forward in your cosplay career.

Hone Your Skills: As you practice the art of cosplay, you'll improve your skills. Polish them until they shine.

Network: Get out and make more cosplay contacts at conventions, local meet-ups, and online forums. You'll make new friends; you'll increase your base of potential colleagues and clients; and you'll learn which cosplay businesses already out there may be hiring.

Share Your Work: Once you've learned the craft, share it! Showcase your work on a website. If you're applying for a job, you can link to that site. If you're working on your own, post information about your work, satisfied customer reviews, and photographs.

When you're ready to build your career in cosplay, it's time to network with others to spread the word about your work.

To sell your creations, check out creative community e-markets like Etsy for crafts, Shapeways for 3D creations, or CosTrader for cosplay items. If you're reluctant to "sell yourself," think of it as sharing your knowledge—and helping beginners!

Keep Going: It will probably take some time to find your dream job or build your own business. As a cosplayer, though, you'll have plenty of practice in patience, planning, and perseverance. You can put that to good use in building a career.

Chapter FIVE

Facing the Future

Will the costumes of the future be interactive and powered by embedded computer chips? Are virtual reality cons on the way? Will you scan your body with a 3D scanner and print out a custom-fitted suit of armor? It may sound like science fiction, but much of what we take for granted today was science fiction a few years ago.

What will happen in the cosplay cosmos over the next five or ten years? No doubt cosplayers will respond innovatively to technological advances, as well as the latest comics, movies, shows, and cartoons. The cosplay community is also likely to be in the vanguard of changing cultural norms and social justice campaigns, within and beyond cosplay. This chapter highlights some developments and career opportunities to look out for, in cosplay and related fields, as cosplay boldly goes into the future.

CHANGES IN FABRICATION AND FASHION

There are many aspects that can change about a material. Prices can fluctuate, depending on where they come from. Technology

Cosplayers develop valuable skills by working with CAD and 3D printers to transform plastic granules like these into cosplay props and other complex objects.

can introduce materials that weren't available before. And consumer needs can impact how fabrics are used. You'll have to keep all of this in mind as you're planning what you need, along with the question of whether or not you will be able to obtain it.

NEW MATERIALS

With the invention and development of new materials, cosplayers have been able to fabricate a previously unimaginable range of costumes and props. Cosplayers work with high-tech materials such as resins, thermoplastics, silicone, and various types of foam. This experience puts cosplayers on the cutting edge of materials science. Perhaps cosplayers will develop the technology to easily produce custom-woven fabrics. Perhaps they'll come up with new ways to build armor or wigs or custom cosmetics. Whatever it is, expect cosplayers to be at the frontiers of materials science in the future.

3D DESIGN AND FABRICATION

As CAD and other computer models are used more widely, cosplayers will design and create more complex costumes and props, and they'll be able to share their models easily with others. The ease of finding construction materials and supplies on the internet will continue to make more cosplay creations accessible to more cosplayers. As the price of 3D printers declines and the quality of 3D-printed objects improves, 3D printing will be more attractive to growing numbers of cosplayers. The cosplay props and costumes of the future will be impressive, indeed.

THE FRONTIERS OF FABRIC

Technology has already made it possible for cosplayers—or anyone—to make custom-designed fabric. All it takes is drawing or painting a design, uploading it to a fabric-printing service, and ordering the fabric you want. An even more impressive technology is e-textiles, or "smart garments." Clothes with electronics and small computers embedded within the fabric can light up or change color. More functionally, e-textiles have the potential to heat and cool the wearer, and researchers are exploring other ways to utilize e-textiles for practical purposes. Technical challenges include waterproofing the electronics and making them less rigid. Expect to see new applications for e-textiles, in cosplay and beyond.

FUTURE FASHION

Clothing makers may respond to the spread of cosplay by designing and selling more everyday cosplay-type fashions.

The Maker Movement

Cosplayers are part of a major global movement: the maker movement. In makerspaces near and far, cosplayers are among those converging to create things. In the maker movement, inventors, designers, and all kinds of do-it-yourselfers have begun designing and making their own creations. The movement brings together techies and technology like 3D printing, alongside nontechies practicing more traditional crafts. From sewing cotton cloth to laser-cutting metal sheets, makers are producing what they want, rather than consuming products made elsewhere. Many makers emphasize reusing or recycling materials that would otherwise be discarded.

As the movement has expanded, gatherings such as Maker Faires have flourished. At a Maker Faire, as many as one hundred thousand or more makers can gather to share information about new maker products, techniques, and technology. Hundreds of Mini Maker Faires have taken place around the world, and this trend seems to be continuing.

Like the maker movement, cosplayers are shaping the future. Making things, whether cosplay or noncosplay, fosters creativity and the ability to solve real-world problems. If you understand how things work, and you've got hands-on experience making things, you're on your way to being an innovator and a problem solver. You can use those skills to enjoy a creative hobby, meet new people, or start a major e-business. Or why not all three?

Ready-to-wear leggings with comic book designs and shirts and dresses paying tribute to superheroes and sci-fi characters have become popular for cosplayers and others. Future fashion designers may push these boundaries further, creating more cosplay-oriented clothing for forward-thinking fashionistas. In fact, that future is already emerging. You or your friends may already be wearing replicas of Hermione Granger's Time-Turner or cool Rebel Alliance jackets.

COSPLAY AND CULTURAL CHANGES

Cosplayers are on the forefront of not only technological developments, but of important social changes, too. Cosplay has a tradition of welcoming everyone.

As new people take up cosplay, they're being increasingly vocal about supporting diversity and inclusion within the cosplay community and beyond.

BUSTING GENDER NORMS

Gender doesn't limit your options when selecting a cosplay. For DC Comics fans, a girl can make herself into a female Joker, or a boy can be a male Wonder Woman. Or, a boy can be Rey from *Star Wars*; a girl can be Luke Skywalker. The latter type of gender-bending costume is called cross-play.

Similarly, don't let gender norms trip you up when you're constructing your costume or props. Do you know a girl who thinks she can't use a saw or a boy who thinks he can't sew? These are skills anyone can learn. Remember, Spider-Man

Gender need not limit a cosplayer's choices. This cosplayer portrays a female Riddler, from DC Comics, at the 2015 New York Comic Con.

sews! Marvel Comics episodes show Peter Parker creating his own Spider-Man costume. Then, after ripping it while combatting crime, he gets out his needle and thread to repair it.

Like other forms of making, sewing is empowering. Todd Burleson, the resource center director of an Illinois elementary school, teaches sewing in his school's makerspace. "I love sewing," he says. "To me it's just another way of creating. I look at it like woodworking. Sewing and woodworking each have unique ways of joining the layers together. The beauty and artistry is in the details. As a man, I love seeing the faces on fellow librarians, teachers and parents when I say I teach sewing in school. It's fun to challenge the stereotype that men don't know how to sew."

This community service volunteer in *Star Wars* gear is visiting with a young patient at a medical center in Thailand.

COMMUNITY SERVICE IN COSPLAY

As cosplay enters the popular culture mainstream, you may see more community service-oriented cosplay activities. Rebel Legion officer Jenna Lindeke Heavenrich explains that today's cosplayers "don't feel like we have to keep our costuming habits 'in the closet' quite so much any more." Rebel Legion's Rebels for a Cause program sends members dressed as *Stars*

Cosplay Is Not Consent: Social Activism and Cosplay

Most of those attending conventions and participating in online forums are supportive of cosplayers, admiring their creations and appreciating the work that went into them. Long-time cosplayer Thea Teufel, who calls herself plus size, has said she appreciates meeting the many cosplayers who are open-minded and accepting.

But as the number of fans has increased, so has an awareness of issues such as sexual harassment among cosplayers. Bullies have attacked both women and men for lacking the "right" body type or race for a cosplayed character. Sexual harassment at conventions has threatened the safety of cosplayers, especially women. These issues have attracted international attention and given rise to antibullying and antiharassment movements in the cosplay community.

The Cosplay Is Not Consent campaign aims to ensure that all conventiongoers understand that wearing a costume is not an invitation for harassment. Nobody is entitled to touch a cosplayer without that person's explicit consent. Similarly, cosplayers with slogans such as Cosplay Is for Everyone! have crusaded on social media and at conventions, supporting the rights of people of any

(continued on the next page)

(continued from the previous page)

size, race, ability, and gender to cosplay the characters of their choice.

At a convention, if you prefer not to be photographed or don't want to pose in a particular way, say so. If you don't want others touching you, let them know. If you encounter bullying or harassment, report it to a convention security officer.

And don't forget to have fun, stick with your friends, and enjoy the cosplay.

Wars characters to hospital visits, walk-a-thons, and other charity events. Other cosplay groups similarly help nonprofit organizations to raise money. The group Carolina Ghostbusters has driven its fully outfitted Ecto-1 Cadillac ambulance to appear at local fundraising events.

Cosplayers have also initiated crusades to address bullying and harassment within the cosplay community. Many cosplayers have worked to make the cosplay community more accessible, including to people of diverse racial and ethnic backgrounds and the LGBTQ community. The current generation of young cosplayers are on their way to becoming leaders in these and other causes they care about.

AN INTERCONNECTED WORLD

The explosion of websites, social media, and new ways to use digital technology to connect affects cosplay in many ways.

For example, proliferating online marketplaces give cosplayers a larger choice of places to buy and sell costumes, props, wigs, and other accessories. As this world of e-commerce expands, there may be new issues of quality control, as low-quality or counterfeit products could flood into the market to meet the demand. Licensing questions may also arise, as media companies that own the rights to certain characters and designs from movies, books, or comics assert their legal claims more aggressively. But the e-commerce expansion is a given.

These cosplayers and friends are celebrating together at a 2016 Club Cosplay event in Anaheim, California. At Club Cosplay, patrons regularly wear their costumes.

Technology has changed the world of publishing, too. With electronic publishing, writers can deliver their words to readers through the internet and e-readers, without going through traditional print publishing companies. Electronic self-publishing has allowed many cosplayers to turn their tutorials and related materials into e-books that are easily accessible online. In this way, experienced cosplayers can help others by sharing the skills they've mastered and also earn money while doing it. As long as the demand for e-published cosplay resources continues, expect to see more e-published books. As more people seek out cosplay information, you may see more traditionally published books in this field, as well.

Overall, the continued expansion of social media will give enterprising cosplayers new ways to spread the word about their businesses and connect with customers. Savvy cosplayers will find ways to use their talents at web design, graphic design, internet advertising, and marketing to find work.

As the internet reaches new populations, more demographics will experience the movies, books, and art forms that cosplay celebrates. New fans may bring cosplay to countries near and far. As Disney put it long ago, it's a small world after all.

So what's next for cosplay? It's clear that the creativity of cosplayers will keep them on the leading edge of popular culture as well as technology. Cosplayers' spirit of experimentation, along with their ability to turn ideas into reality, gives them the capability to design and create objects that we haven't even thought of yet. It also enables them to envision and work toward a better community and a more just world.

Let's see what's out there!

Glossary

anime A style of animated film or show that originated in Japan, using bright colors, strong characters, action-filled plots, and often futuristic themes.

computer-aided design (CAD) The use of computer programs and technology to create or modify plans, patterns, or inventions that are often three dimensional.

convention A large meeting of people coming together, usually for several days, to discuss a common interest or shared work; sometimes abbreviated to "con," as in "Comic Con."

cosplay Dressing up to portray characters from fiction (especially science fiction, fantasy, manga, and anime) or sometimes historical characters; can be used as a verb.

costuming Making, and often wearing, outfits from a particular time period or culture for historical reenactment, theatrical or movie productions, or for appearances at conventions and other events.

digital Electronic and especially computerized technology.

e-commerce The buying and selling of goods and services over the internet.

fabricate To make, construct, or build something from raw materials.

fantasy Imaginative fiction, often featuring strange settings, grotesque characters, and magical worlds.

freecycle To divert waste from landfills by giving unwanted items, for free, to others who want them.

internship A temporary and usually short-term position in which someone offers their labor in exchange for relevant job experience and skills.

LGBTQ A collective term for people who identify as lesbian, gay, bisexual, transgender, and/or queer/questioning.

makerspace A place where people gather to invent and build, using hardware and software tools such as sewing machines, computers, 3D printers, and craft or construction materials.

manga A style of comic book or graphic novel originating in Japan, with a range of stories including action-adventure and romance.

marketing Activities undertaken to make people aware of a product or service.

masquerade A gathering of people in costume that may involve a contest.

networking Exchanging information in order to develop productive business relationships.

robotics The processes and technology involved with the design, construction, and operation of robots.

science fiction Invented stories dealing with the influence of real or invented scientific developments on people and society.

solder To melt metal or metallic alloy in order to join or fuse two or more metallic surfaces or pieces.

For More Information

Academy of Art University
79 New Montgomery Street
San Francisco, CA 94105
(800) 544-2787
Website: http://www.academyart.edu

Academy of Art University offers academic programs including online classes, a high school diploma program, and degrees. Topics of study include acting, advertising, animation and visual effects, architecture, fashion, fine art, game development, and more.

Comic-Con International: San Diego
PO Box 128458
San Diego, CA 92112
(619) 414-1020
Website: http://www.comic-con.org

Comic-Con International: San Diego is a nonprofit educational organization dedicated to creating awareness of, and appreciation for, comics and related art forms, primarily through conventions and similar events.

EMP Museum at Seattle Center
325 5th Avenue N
Seattle, WA 98109
(206) 770-2700
Website: http://www.empmuseum.org

EMP, a museum devoted to music, science fiction, and popular culture, is the site of the Science Fiction and Fantasy Hall of Fame. It hosts music events and competitions, a film festival focused on science fiction, fantasy, and horror, a sci-fi and fantasy writing contest, and the Seattle Mini Maker Faire.

Fab Foundation
50 Milk Street, 16th floor
Boston, MA 02109
(857) 333-7777
Email: info@fabfoundation.org
Website: http://www.fabfoundation.org/about-us/

The Fab Foundation works towards enabling anyone to make (almost) anything, creating opportunities to improve people's lives around the world. It works with community organizations and educational institutions to provide access to the tools, knowledge, and financial means to innovate and invent tangible goods using technology and digital fabrication.

FIRST (For Inspiration & Recognition of Science & Technology)
200 Bedford Street
Manchester, NH 03101
(603) 666-3906 or (800) 871-8326
Website: http://www.firstinspires.org

A nonprofit organization, FIRST seeks to inspire young people to become leaders in science and technology. It sponsors mentor-based research and robotics programs, including robotics competitions and LEGO leagues.

FIRST Robotics Canada
PO Box 518
Pickering Main
Pickering, ON L1V2R7
Canada
Website: http://www.firstroboticscanada.org

This organization supports young Canadians who are interested in careers in science, technology, and engineering. It also sponsors scholarships, teams, robotics competitions, and LEGO leagues.

International Game Developers Association
19 Mantua Road
Mt. Royal, NJ 08061
Website: https://www.igda.org

IGDA is a nonprofit membership organization serving individuals, including students, from all around the world who make games.

National Costumers Association (NCA)
6000 E. Evans Avenue, #3-205
Denver, CO 80222
(800) 622-1321
Website: http://www.costumers.org

The NCA promotes the art of costuming and offers student scholarships, a quarterly newsletter, internships, mentorships, and business opportunities.

National Theater School of Canada
5030 St. Denis Street
Montreal, QC H2J 2L8
Canada
(866) 547-7328 (Canada and United States) or (514) 842-7954
Website: https://ent-nts.ca/en/

The National Theater School of Canada offers instruction in acting, directing, production, and playwriting, as well as a program in costume and set design.

Society of Illustrators
128 East 63rd Street
New York, NY 10065
(212) 838-2560
Website: http://www.societyillustrators.org

The Society of Illustrators is a professional organization for
illustrators that is dedicated to promoting the art of
illustration. The society hosts two museums: the Museum of
Comic and Cartoon Art and the Museum of American
Illustration.

WEBSITES

Because of the changing nature of internet links, Rosen Publishing
has developed an online list of websites related to the subject of
this book. This site is updated regularly. Please use this link to
access this list:

http://www.rosenlinks.com/TTHIC/cosplay

For Further Reading

Bernier, Samuel N., Bertier Luyt, and Tatiana Reinhard. *Design for 3D Printing: Scanning, Creating, Editing, Remixing and Making in Three Dimensions.* San Francisco, CA: Maker Media, Inc., 2015.

Ceceri, Kathy. *Making Simple Robots: Exploring Cutting-Edge Robotics with Everyday Stuff.* San Francisco, CA: Maker Media, Inc., 2015.

Chenery, Craig W. *The Comicon & Convention Survival Guide.* Pop Culture Planet Publishing, 2015.

Cline, Lydia. *3D Printing with Autodesk 123D, Tinkercad, and MakerBot.* New York, NY: McGraw-Hill Education, 2015.

Creative Publishing International. *First Time Sewing: The Absolute Beginner's Guide.* Minneapolis, MN: Creative Publishing International, 2014.

Crossland, Samantha R. *Steampunk & Cosplay: Fashion Design & Illustration.* Lake Forest, CA: Walter Foster, 2015.

Day, Felicia. *You're Never Weird on the Internet.* New York, NY: Touchstone, 2015.

Doran, Bill. *Foamsmith: How to Create Foam Armor Costumes.* Bill Doran, e-book; print 2015.

Gatcum, Chris. *The Beginner's Photography Guide.* New York, NY: DK Publishing, 2013.

Han, Yaya, Allison DeBlasio, and Joey Marsocci. *1,000 Incredible Costume and Cosplay Ideas: A Showcase of Creative Characters from Anime, Manga, Video Games, Comics, and More.* Beverly, MA: Quarry Books, 2013.

Krix, Harrison. *Painting and Weathering for Props and Replicas.* Krix Harrison, e-book.

LeLarge, Blandine. *Fashion Design Lookbook: More Than 50 Creative Tips and Techniques for the Fashion-Forward Artist.* Irvine, CA: Walter Foster, 2014.

Pawlewski, Sarah. *Careers: The Graphic Guide to Finding the Perfect Career for You.* New York, NY: DK Publishing, 2015.

Poolos, Jamie. *Careers in Online Gaming.* New York, NY: Rosen Publishing, 2014.

Quindt, Svetlana. *The Book of Cosplay Lights: Getting Started with LEDs.* Svetlanda Quindt, e-book.

Takasou, Yuki, Rumine, and Kashiko Kurobuchi. *Cosplay Basics: A Beginners Guide to the Art of Costume Play.* Long Island City, NY: One Peace Books, 2015.

Tash, Sarvenaz. *The Geek's Guide to Unrequited Love.* New York, NY: Simon & Schuster, 2016.

Vescia, Monique. *A Teen's Guide to the Power of Social Networking: Social Network-Powered Employment Opportunities.* New York, NY: Rosen Publishing, 2014.

Willett, Edward. *Career Building Through Using Digital Design Tools.* New York, NY: Rosen Publishing, 2014.

Willoughby, Nick. *Digital Filmmaking for Kids for Dummies.* Hoboken, NJ: John Wiley & Sons, Inc., 2015.

Bibliography

Ashcraft, Brian, and Luke Plunkett. *Cosplay World*. New York, NY: Prestel, 2014.

Bajarin, Tim. "Why the Maker Movement is Important to America's Future." *Time.* May 19, 2014. http://time.com/104210/maker-faire-maker-movement.

Burleson, Todd. Interview by e-mail with author. May 2016.

Cardenas, Richard. "Meet the Cast: SyFy's *Heroes of Cosplay* — Jessica Merizan & Holly Conrad." PopCults Geek and Alternative Pop Culture. August 12, 2013. http://www.popcults.com/meet-the-cast-syfys-heroes-of-cosplay-jessica-merizan-holly-conrad.

Donahue, Caroline. Interview with the author. April 2016.

Hadfield, James. "What's beneath all that latex, fabric and plastic?" *Japan Times*. December 6, 2014. http://www.japantimes.co.jp/culture/2014/12/06/books/whats-beneath-latex-fabric-plastic/#.VylqVmM3crc.

Han, Yaya. "Bio." YayaHan.com. Retrieved May 4, 2016. http://yayahan.com/about.

James, Will. "GeekDad Interviews Foamsmithing Master Bill Doran." GeekDad. May 15, 2015. https://geekdad.com/2015/05/bill-doran.

Kreneck, Todd. "Cosplay Boom: Origins, Parts 1 and 2." September 30, 2014. https://www.youtube.com/watch?v=J62cdAob9_I&feature=youtu.be.

Kroski, Ellyssa. "A Librarian's Guide to Makerspaces: 16 Resources." Open Education Database. March 12, 2013. http://oedb.org/ilibrarian/a-librarians-guide-to-makerspaces.

Lindeke Heavenrich, Jenna. A series of e-mail exchanges with the author. April–May 2016.

Maggs, Sam. *The Fangirl's Guide to the Galaxy.* Philadelphia, PA: Quirk Books, 2015.

Quindt, Svetlana. "About Me." Kamui Cosplay. Retrieved May 3, 2016. https://www.kamuicosplay.com.

Renfaire.com. "What is Faire?" Renfaire.com. Retrieved April 23, 2016. http://www.renfaire.com/General/faire.html.

Romano, Andrea. "Cosplay Is Not Consent: The People Fighting Sexual Harassment at Comic Con." Mashable. October 15, 2014. http://mashable.com/2014/10/15/new -york-comic-con-harassment/#.JriTjqxsPqU.

Savage, Steven. *Focused Fandom: Cosplay, Costuming, and Careers.* Charleston, SC: CreateSpace, 2013.

Society for Creative Anachronism. "Society Seneschal." Retrieved April 19, 2016. http://socsen.sca.org/society -chatelaine/newcomer-resources-and-information.

Stager, Gary. "What's the Maker Movement and Why Should I Care?" Scholastic.com. Retrieved May 8, 2016. http://www .scholastic.com/browse/article.jsp?id=3758336.

Takahara, Miyuu, and Kenji Weston. *Cosplay—The Beginner's Masterclass: A Guide to Cosplay Culture & Costume Making: Finding Materials, Planning, Ideas, How to Make Clothing, Props & Enjoy Conventions.* Charleston, SC: CreateSpace, 2015.

Yang, Jeff. "The Cosplay's the Thing." SF Gate. April 8, 2009. http://www.sfgate.com/entertainment/article/The-Cosplay -s-the-Thing-2480710.php.

Index

ABOUT THE AUTHOR

Christy Mihaly, a confirmed Trekkie and enthusiastic Potterhead, began writing long ago, though not in a galaxy far, far away. She has published articles, stories, poetry, and nonfiction books for readers of all ages, from preschool through adult. In her younger days, she sewed much of her own wardrobe, although nowadays her daughters can knit circles around her. Mihaly's research for this book and the many delightful cosplayers she met deepened her appreciation for the artistry and energy of the wonderful world of cosplay. She especially wishes to thank Caroline Donahue, Jenna Lindeke Heavenrich, and Todd Burleson for their contributions to this book.

PHOTO CREDITS

Cover © iStockphoto.com/Nancy Nehring; p. 5 Daniel Knighton/FilmMagic/Getty Images; pp. 8, 49 © AP Images; p. 10 Charley Gallay/Getty Images; p. 15 Chamille White/Shutterstock.com; pp. 18, 50 DreamPictures/Blend Images/Getty Images; p. 20 Bruce Laurance/The Image Bank/Getty Images; p. 22 Lisa Maree Williams/Getty Images; p. 24 Westend61/Getty Images; p. 27 Blend Images – Hill Street Studios/Brand X Pictures/Getty Images; p. 30 wavebreakmedia/Shutterstock.com; p. 32 StockPhotosArt/Shutterstock.com; p. 34 Philippe Lopez/AFP/Getty Images; p. 38 Robertus Pudyanto/Getty Images; p. 42 Anadolu Agency/Getty Images; p. 44 © The Orange County Register/ZUMA Press; p. 54 Monkey Business Images/Shutterstock.com; p. 57 Aykut Erdogdu/Shutterstock.com; p. 61 Daniel Zuchnik/Getty Images; p. 62 Pacific Press/LightRocket/Getty Images; p. 65 Albert L. Ortega/Getty Images; back cover and interior pages background image Vladgrin/Shutterstock.com.

Designer: Nicole Russo; Editor: Bernadette Davis;
Photo Researcher: Karen Huang

From Taxis to Skyscrapers

by Joyce Markovics

Consultant: Kimberly Brenneman, PhD
National Institute for Early Education Research, Rutgers University
New Brunswick, New Jersey

New York, New York

Credits

Cover, © Eldad Carin/Shutterstock, © Rawpixel/Shutterstock, © Space Chimp/ Shutterstock, and © Bruno Ferrari/Shutterstock; 3T, © Martin Shields/Alamy; 3M, © justasc/Shutterstock; 3B, © iStock/Thinkstock; 4–5, © Songquan Deng/Shutterstock; 6, © 1000 Words/Shutterstock; 7, © Ian Hubball/Thinkstock; 8–9, © Bruno Ferrari/ Shutterstock; 10–11, © Songquan Deng/Thinkstock; 12, © Tony Tallec/Alamy; 13, © Sascha Preussner/Shutterstock; 14–15, © iStock/Thinkstock; 16–17, © Kuttig–Travel/Alamy; 18–19, © Martin Shields/Alamy; 19, © rorem/Shutterstock; 20, © dashingstock/Shutterstock; 21, © Scott Cornell/Shutterstock; 22T, © iStock/ Thinkstock; 22B, © stockelements/Shutterstock; 23TL, © Mike Flippo/Shutterstock; 23TR, © 123RF; 23BL, © iStock/Thinkstock; 23BR, © Debby Wong/Shutterstock; 24, © Tom Grundy.

Publisher: Kenn Goin
Senior Editor: Joyce Tavolacci
Creative Director: Spencer Brinker
Design: Debrah Kaiser
Photo Researcher: Michael Win

Library of Congress Cataloging-in-Publication Data

Markovics, Joyce L., author.
  City colors : from taxis to skyscrapers / by Joyce Markovics.
      pages cm.—(Colors tell a story)
  Includes bibliographical references and index.
  ISBN-13: 978-1-62724-322-3 (library binding)
  ISBN-10: 1-62724-322-4 (library binding)
  1. Colors—Juvenile literature. 2. Cities and towns—Juvenile literature. I. Title.
QC495.5.M3675 2015
535.6—dc23

For more information, write to Bearport Publishing Company, Inc., 45 West 21st Street, Suite 3B, New York, New York 10010. Printed in the United States of America.

10 9 8 7 6 5 4 3 2 1

Contents

City Colors

Cities are full of bright, bold colors.

They tell an exciting story about the city.

A **traffic light** turns red.

Cars and buses screech to a halt.

Red means stop.

7

A yellow car whizzes by.

The color lets people know it's a taxi.

The car drops off one person
and picks up another.

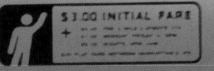

$3.00 INITIAL FARE

The top of a tall building shines with bright lights.

The lights are red, white, and blue.

That's because it's the Fourth of July!

11

A person rushes down a hall in a hospital.

She is dressed in green.

The color lets people know she's a doctor.

The city sky changes from morning to night.

During the day, it's bright blue.

As the sun sets, the sky turns orange.

15

Look at the white stripes on the busy road.

They form a crosswalk.

The white stripes tell people where it's safe to cross the street.

A **subway** map uses many colors.

Each color shows a different subway **route**.

Each route travels between different places.

People in a parade march in colorful **uniforms**.

Big balloons float
down the street.

Look at all the
city's colors!

Explore More:
A Skyscraper's Colors

The Empire State Building is a famous skyscraper in New York City. The top of the building changes color to celebrate different holidays.

Look at the pictures. Each one shows the Empire State Building during a different holiday. Think about the colors that represent the holidays listed below, and then match each picture with the correct holiday.

1. Valentine's Day

2. St. Patrick's Day

3. Thanksgiving

4. Hanukkah

5. Christmas

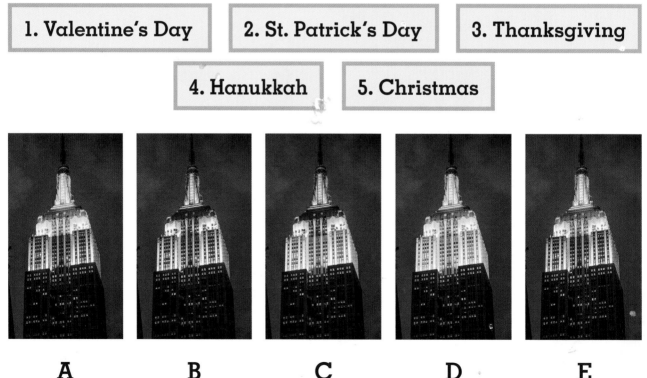

A   B   C   D   E

22

Answers are on page 24.

Glossary

route (ROOT) the road or path a person or train follows to get from one place to another

subway (SUHB-way) an electric train or system of trains that runs underground in a city

traffic light (TRAF-ik LITE) a set of lights that controls traffic

uniforms (YOO-nuh-forms) special sets of clothes worn by a group

23

Index

Read More

Milich, Zoran. *City Colors.* Toronto: Kids Can Press (2006).

Wellington, Monica. *Colors for Zena.* New York: Dial Books (2013).

Learn More Online

To learn more about city colors, visit
www.bearportpublishing.com/ColorsTellaStory

About the Author

Joyce Markovics and her husband, Adam, live along the Hudson River in Tarrytown, New York. Joyce works in bright, bold, and colorful New York City.

Answers to Page 22:

1. B; 2. D; 3. E; 4. C; 5. A